Bohemian Macramé

Bohemian Macramé

Gwenaël Petiot

LARK

New York

An Imprint of Sterling Publishing Co., Inc.
1166 Avenue of the Americas
New York, NY 10036

Book design: Ned Hoste/2H Design

ISBN 978-1-4547-0986-2

Distributed in Canada by Sterling Publishing Co., Inc.
c/o Canadian Manda Group, 664 Annette Street
Toronto, Ontario, Canada M6S 2C8

For information about custom editions, specials sales, and premium and corporate purchase, please contact Sterling Special Sales at 800-805-5489 or specialsales@sterlingpublishing.com

Manufactured in China

2 4 6 8 10 9 7 5 3 1

www.sterlingpublishing.com

www.larkcrafts.com

Contents

Projects

p.58

p.78

p.72

p.104

Introduction

Macramé is an old knotting technique for creating textiles out of cords or string. There are different theories about its origin, but the most accepted is that it was devised by 13th century North African weavers. The word "macramé" itself comes from the Arabic word "migramah," which in turn means "ornamental fringe." North African artisans brought their skills, including macramé, to Spain during the Moorish conquest of the Iberian peninsula in the 8th century.

By the end of the 19th century, macramé had become a predominantly decorative art commonly used to create and embellish tablecloths, bedspreads, and even curtains. In the 20th century, particularly in the 1960s and 1970s, macramé became especially popular in America and Europe, propelled by the interest in handmade crafts popularized by the hippy movement. Household items like plant hangers, elaborate wall hangings—such as the ubiquitous macramé owl—plus jewelry items like bracelets and necklaces were widely made before the craft gradually dwindled in popularity. However, the beginning of the 21st century has seen a renewed interest in crafts and macramé in particular, especially in the high-end jewelry and fashion worlds, where bohemian-style clothes and ornaments such as belts, sandals, and anklets have become desirable objects.

I discovered the art of macramé in South America. There it's a popular craft and is still an intrinsic part of the culture. I was amazed by the different creative possibilities given by using only cords and knots, and more than anything, I thoroughly enjoyed creating something unique and personal. I cannot imagine having better teachers than my Peruvian and Argentine craftsman friends, and I'm delighted to continue sharing this limitless handcraft with you through this book.

By following my instructions, you will be able to create your own bohemian macramé. Don't be put off by the complexity of some projects—it actually only takes a few different knots to do all of these creations. Above all, carefully read the knots section and patiently practice every knot to thoroughly master it before starting a project. Don't hesitate to change the cord, cord color, or bead disposition to personalize your work. After some practice you will be able to create your own designs by mixing the knot combinations. But don't jump between steps! Learning the basics is the tricky part—you will make mistakes, but everyone does. Just be patient and follow the steps carefully.

Now let's knot!

Materials

Macramé requires very few tools. Here is a list of the basic supplies you will need to follow the step-by-step projects:

HOLDING BOARD + CLIPS

You will need one holding board plus at least two clips. These are necessary to secure your knotting and to hold individual knots correctly. You can use a board made of wood, plastic, or even cardboard from a strong carton. The clips help you to easily move the macramé creation in any direction and block it (stop it moving) while you are tying the knots.

In some projects, you will need a holding board cord. This is a cord that you'll clip horizontally to your board to hold the project cords. In most cases the color of the cord does not matter as it is pulled off when the knotting is done, but it does have to be as long as the board is wide.

ADVICE

I strongly suggest that you carefully read each of the Step-by-Step sections before starting the project itself so as to completely understand each stage. Taken bit by bit and broken down into pieces, even complicated instructions become much easier.

SKILL LEVELS

The number of beads indicates difficulty:
- ● beginner
- ●● intermediary
- ●●● expert

C&M

Used in every project, this abbreviation means Cut and Melt (or burn) the excess cords. See the **Lighter** section on page 4 for details.

MACRAMÉ CORDS

You can use any type of cord or cords to do macramé, including cotton, wool, hemp, silk, jute, or even leather, plus synthetic cords such as nylon or polyester.

Personally, I like to use waxed polyester cords: These can be melted after cutting the cord ends on completion of a creation. It gives a great finish to your pieces; it's flexible and very strong at the same time; there are many colors; and it's very reasonably priced. Most of the waxed polyester cords are 1mm thick, which is both perfect for incorporating beads easily and the ideal size to do detailed macramé jewelry. Also, the wax makes the creations stiff and waterproof, which is great when you wear your macramé bracelets every day, as I do. These are also the kind of cords you need to use if you want to recreate the exact same pieces in my step-by-step projects.

CABOCHONS

A cabochon is an oval-shaped ornament with a domed surface and flat bottom. It's usually a gemstone or semi-precious stone, but it can also be made of resin, wood, or glass. The most common shape is round or oval, but you can also find rectangular or even teardrop-shaped cabochons. In this book I have used tiger eye, malachite, turquoise, chrysocolla, labradorite, and red jasper cabochons.

BEADS

Incorporating beads in macramé jewelry is an easy and attractive way to embellish your creations. Beads can be found in a wide variety of different materials, but in this book I mainly use copper beads as well as stone beads, such as turquoise, amethyst, or lapis lazuli. Most of them measure between 2mm and 6mm.

When you choose beads, you **must** first check that the hole diameter is big enough to pass your cord through.

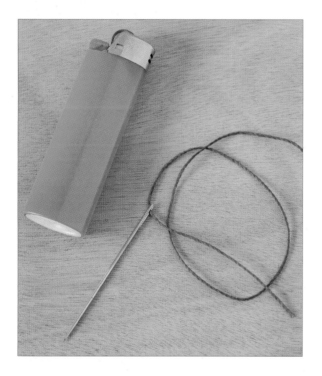

LIGHTER

Synthetic cords need to be cauterized after you cut them at the end of the project so that the last knots do not loosen and untie themselves over time. Cord burners are especially made for this kind of handicraft, but a simple lighter is good enough.

Once you finish a project, cut the cord remains, leaving one or two millimeters, and burn or melt (C&M) the extremity for a couple of seconds. Wait a few seconds to be sure you don't burn yourself, then lightly press on it to fix the weld. Natural cords will not melt; instead you will have to use glue to secure the knots. Cut the cord close to the last knot, leaving just enough length to put a drop of glue on, then cut and secure the end.

NEEDLE

You don't need a special needle to make macramé. Just be sure the eye of the needle is big enough to pass your cord through.

RULER AND SCISSORS

A ruler is useful for measuring the strings before starting a project. Alternatively, you can also use a measuring tape, which makes things easier when you need to cut long cords. Small scissors with good sharp, fine tips are necessary to cut the cord cleanly.

EARRING HOOKS & METAL JUMP RINGS

I recommend avoiding any metal containing nickel for earring hooks because it can cause allergic reactions in many people. It's much better to use surgical steel, though sometimes even this can contain a small percentage of nickel. If you are very sensitive to metal, consider using copper or silver hooks. Alternatively, earring hooks and metal jump rings are also easily made with simple wire wrap techniques.

PLIERS

A round or flat-nose pair of pliers is invaluable for opening and closing metal jump rings and attaching hooks to macramé earrings.

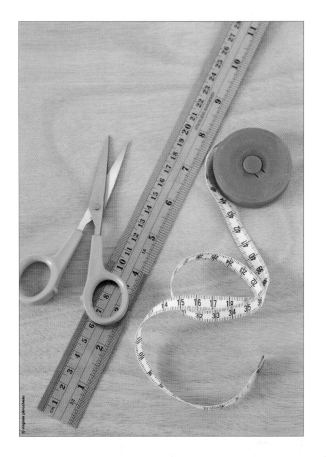

Knots

This section will help you learn about different knots and macramé techniques—such as how to wrap a stone. To understand macramé knots, you need to first comprehend the difference between the holding cord and the knotting cord.

The **holding cord** is the cord you use to tie the knot around. It is the foundation of the work and is sometimes called the knot bearer. It gives the direction of your line, and when the work is complete, it is usually completely hidden inside the macramé. It is important that it holds firm and steady when making a knot.

The **knotting cord** is simply the thread you use to actually make the knot and is part of the project itself. This is the moving cord. However, the holding and knotting cords can change positions through the pattern; a cord that is the holding cord in one step can become the knotting cord in another step. It may look confusing, but don't worry—practice all the basic knots several times until you consistently make regular neat knots. Knowing each knot perfectly will make things a lot easier when you start your step-by-step projects!

Overhand Knot

This is the easiest macramé knot—this is the knot we all learned to tie our shoes with when we were kids. It's usually used to install the cords before starting, to add a color row in the pattern, or to secure the beads. To tie this knot, hold the cord in both hands, make a loop (Step 1), bring one end through the loop, and pull on both ends (Step 2).

Single Half Hitch Knot

A single half hitch knot is very similar to the overhand knot. Make a loop, but instead of using just one cord, use two; one as the holding cord, and the other as the knotting cord. In this book the single half hitch knot is always followed by a second one. This makes a double half hitch knot.

Lark's Head Knot (and **Reverse Lark's Head Knot**)

As with the overhand knot, the lark's head knot is usually used for preparation stages before starting the macramé. To practice this knot, you need a holding board with a horizontally secured cord. Fold the knotting cord in half and place it under the holding cord with the folded part at the bottom and the two ends at the top (Step 1). Bring both ends over the holding cord and pass them under the folding loop (Step 2), then pull both ends together to tie the knot (Step 3). To do a reverse lark's head knot, pass the knotting cord under the holding cord with both ends facing you. Bring the folded section above the holding cord, pass the two ends over the loop, and pull them.

Horizontal and Diagonal Double Half Hitch Knot

The double half hitch knot is one of the most ubiquitous knots in macramé. It can be made horizontally, vertically, and diagonally, and all directions need to be practiced. When I talk about "line" in the step-by-step projects, this is the knot you need. To make it easier to follow in the photos, I used a blue thread for the holding cord and lime green for the knotting cords.

To make a line from right to left: Firmly pull the holding cord with your left hand in the opposite direction (Step 1), while with the right hand, loop the next cord, passing it under then over the holding cord, then finally inside the loop above itself. Pull on it, and your single half hitch knot is done. Make a similar loop with the same cord to complete your knot. By tying a series of double half hitch knots with several knotting cords, a line shape will form (Step 4).

To make a line from left to right: Use your right hand to tense the holding cord, and with your left hand, make the loops in exactly the same way (Step 6).

The diagonal double half hitch knot is tied exactly the same way as the horizontal one, except that the holding cord is held at a diagonal angle.

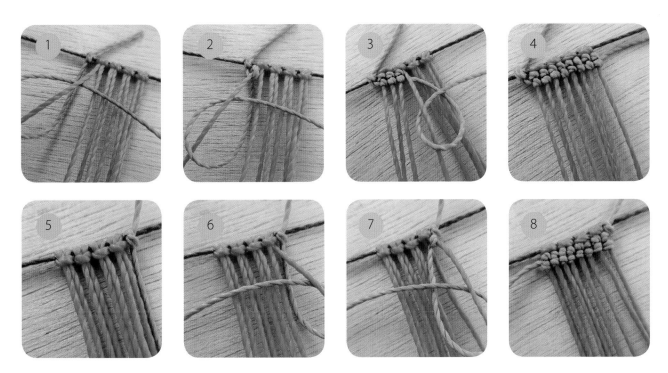

Vertical Double Half Hitch Knot

This knot uses just one knotting cord to make knots on several holding cords. To make the explanation clearer, I have shown the knotting cord in green and the holding cords in red. When I talk about doing a "row," this is the kind of knot you have to use in the step-by-step projects.

To make a vertical knot, make a loop with the knotting cord, passing it under then over the holding cord and then inside the loop above it (Step 1). Do this twice (Step 2). Before tying the second half of the knot, be sure the first loop is tightly placed against the previous knot. This vertical double knot is repeated each time, using the next thread as the holding cord until the end of the row (Steps 3 and 4). The top row of pictures shows the row working from left to right, and the lower row shows knotting from right to left.

Square Knot or Flat Knot

String a holding cord across the board, then fix three knotting cords with simple overhand knots at each extremity. To simplify the explanation, I have used cords in two colors: the knotting cords are brown and the holding cord is blue (Step 1). In some projects, you will be instructed to do this knot with two holding cords, which means two cords inside the knot, but the way to do it will be exactly the same, just with two cords.

Move the left knotting cord over the holding cord to create a loop and then under the right thread (Step 2). Then the right thread goes under the holding cord and comes up in the loop over the left cord (Step 3). Pull on both ends to tie the knot (Step 4). The first half of the knot is done—this is a half square knot.

To complete the knot, repeat the first step, but this time make the first loop using the right thread. Move it over the holding cord then under the left knotting cord (Step 5). Then pass the left cord under the holding cord and bring it up in the loop (Step 6). Pull on both ends to complete the full square knot (Step 7). Repeated square knots create a flat braid pattern (Step 8).

To make a neat knot, the holding cord needs to have tension: This can be achieved by fixing it tightly with a clip onto the board or holding it between the teeth while the knot is tied. I personally prefer the latter because the tension can be adjusted quickly and easily, and it's much more practical than moving the clip every time a different holding cord is used.

Spiral Square Knot

If half square knots are repeated over and over—meaning that the first loop on the same side is used every time a knot is made—a spiral pattern will emerge. It makes no difference whether this is started on the right or left side.

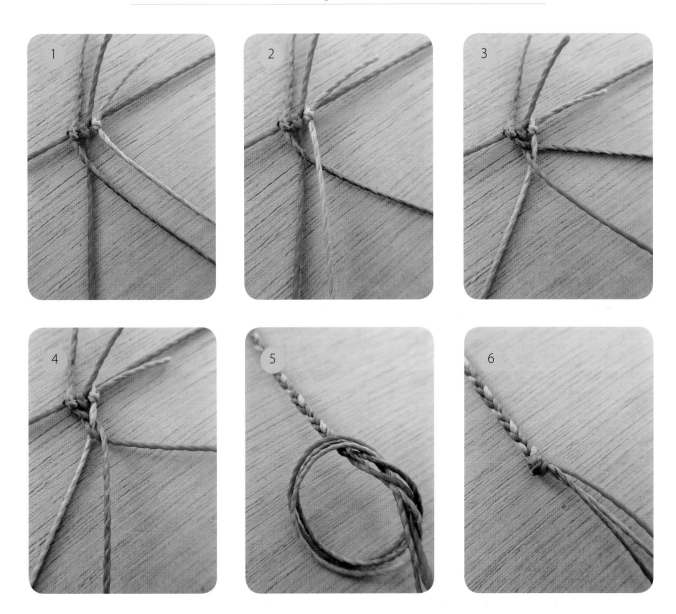

How to make a three-strand braid

Clip a holding cord horizontally to the board; fix three strands with simple overhand knots at each extremity. Bring the left strand over the center strand (Step 1), then the right strand over the center strand (Step 2). Successively keep moving the outer cords into the center (Steps 3 and 4). Hold the cords under tension as the plait progresses to get a neat result. At the required length, secure the plait, making a tight overhand knot using all three cords at the same time (Steps 5 and 6).

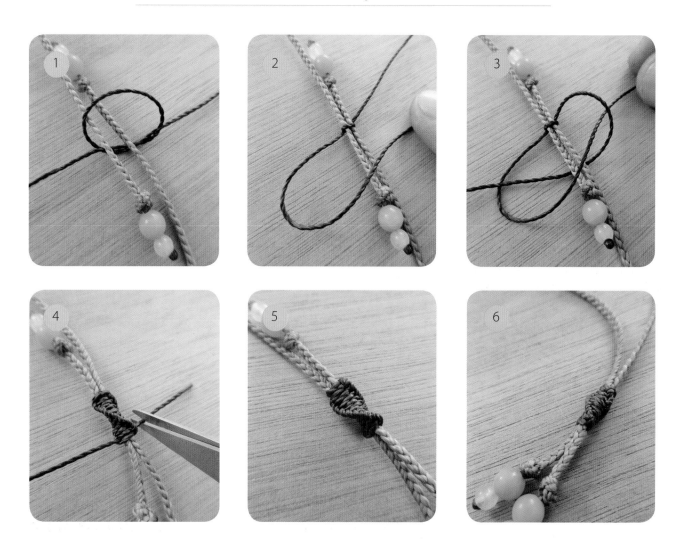

How to make a sliding clasp

When finishing a bracelet or necklace, a sliding clasp will
be needed to hold the braids. This clasp also helps with the
adjustment of jewelry.

Take a 10-inch (25 cm) piece of cord and knot it in the middle
with a simple overhand knot around the two braids (Step 1).
With both braids as holding cords, tie several spiral square knots
(Steps 2 and 3) until your sliding clasp is long enough. I usually
like to use ten knots (Step 4). Don't tie the knots too tightly—the
knot needs to slide easily when finished. When the knots are
done, C&M the remaining cord lengths. (Step 5).

Depending on the project, both braids can be "going" in the
same direction (Step 6).

How to wrap a cabochon

This method is for wrapping a cabochon or any medallion-shaped object using cord.

Apart from the holding cord across the board, only three strands are needed to do the wrapping—two holding cords and one knotting cord (Step 1). The knotting cord length has to be at least 12 times the size of the stone perimeter; in this example my stone measures about 3½ inches (9 cm), so I am using a 43-inch (110 cm) orange cord.

To make this easier to follow, I used a second color for the holding cords, but try to practice it with the same color. The strand length has to be at least four times the stone perimeter; here I am using two 15½-inch (39 cm) brown cords.

Tie both holding cords with simple overhand knots, leaving about 6 inches (15 cm) of cord above the holding cord. Separate the cords a little wider than the thickness of the stone; about ¼-inch (6 mm) wider the first few times you wrap the stone and less after some practice (Step 2).

Incorporate the knotting cord by making a simple overhand knot into the right holding cord (Step 3), and complete its placing by adding one vertical half hitch knot from right to left (Step 4).

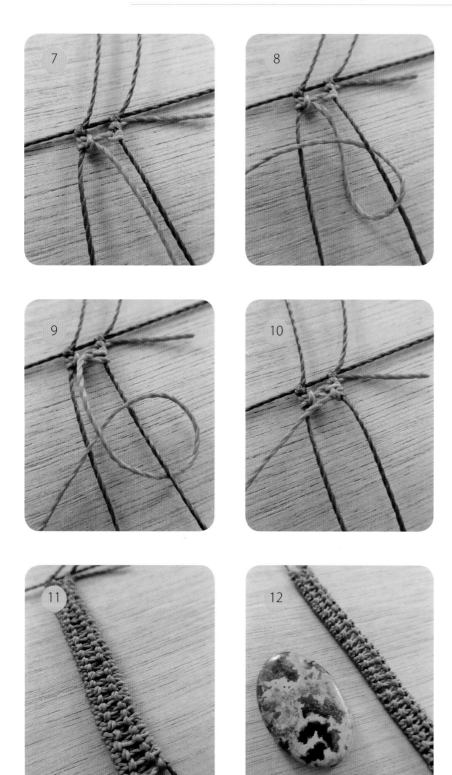

Next make a loop, passing it above and then under the left cord, and finally over itself (Step 5). Tie this first half knot gently to maintain the spacing between the holding cords. To complete the knot, make another loop, passing the knotting cord under then over the left cord, and inside the loop under itself. Tighten (Steps 6 and 7).

Do the same knot on the right side as on the left, just inverting the method: Make the first loop, passing the knotting cord above and then under the right cord, and finally inside the loop above itself (Step 8). Complete the knot by making the second loop, passing it under then over the right cord, and inside the loop under itself (Steps 9 and 10).

Continue the same knot over and over, left and right, until the length of the wrapping covers three-quarters of the stone perimeter. Be sure to make the last knot on the right holding cord (Step 11). Check the gap between the holding cords with your stone every five knots to be sure it stays equal during the weaving.

Untie both overhand knots made at the beginning, and space out the wrapping knots so they slide and finally cover the whole stone perimeter (Step 12).

Next comes the tricky part! Wrap the stone with the net weave, and knot both ends of the left holding cord together on the front side of the stone with a double half hitch knot (Step 13). Be careful not to make the knot too tight. Turn over the stone and repeat the knot with the ends of the right holding cord (Step 14); do this as delicately as possible at the beginning! Flip the stone over several times to adjust the tension on both knots until they are finally both tightened very firmly.

Now the objective is to pass both front cords on the cabochon to the back; the ends need to be hidden so that the sealing will not be visible from the front.

Working on the back, knot the lower-left cord around the upper left cord with a tight double half hitch knot (Step 15). Repeat the same knots with the right strands (Step 16). Finally, cut the cords, leaving a couple of millimeters (Step 17), and carefully C&M the extremities (Step 18).

The glue-free macramé wrapping is done.

Diamond-Shaped Earrings

Macramé strands

Two teal blue, 12 inches (30 cm)

Six navy blue, 14 inches (36 cm)

Four beige, 6 inches (15 cm)

One holding cord the width of the board

Materials

Two 6-mm pink quartz stone beads

Four 3-mm sodalite stone beads

Two 4-mm metal jump rings

Two earring hooks

Pliers

Knotting board + clips

Scissors

Ruler & lighter

These casual, summery earrings are an ideal first project to introduce the art of macramé.

Dimensions: The diamond is 1¼ inches (3 cm) long; overall the earrings measure 2 inches (5 cm), including the stone beads

Required Knots: Lark's head knot, diagonal and vertical double half hitch knot, overhand knot

Diamond-Shaped Earrings

STEP 1 Clip the holding cord horizontally across the board (the color does not matter as it is pulled off once the knotting is complete). Fold in half and install three navy-blue cords using lark's head knots. Then, with simple overhand knots, tie one beige cord on each side of the farthest left navy-blue knot and one teal-blue cord between the other two navy-blue knots.

STEP 2 Working from right to left, create the first diagonal line with double half hitch knots; the holding cord is the first navy-blue cord on the right.

STEP 3 Repeat the previous step to make a second line using the first navy-blue cord on the right. At the end of this second line, knot the last navy-blue strand—this is the one used as the holding cord on the first line.

STEP 4 Hold the teal-blue cord with your left hand and tie vertical double half hitch knots on every strand all the way across the last line. At the end, knot the last navy-blue thread—the one previously used as the holding cord.

STEP 5 Repeat Steps 2 and 3 to make two final diagonal lines going from right to left with double half hitch knots, again using the farthest right cords as holding cords.

STEP 6 Knot a second earring, repeating every step as before. Pull off your holding cord when both earrings are done.

STEP 7 Cut every strand, trim carefully, and C&M the ends— except the strand used as the holding cord to make the last line. This is used for the stone beads and to attach the ear hook.

STEP 8 Add the stone beads as shown in the picture to create the same earrings, or be creative and personalize them. Tie an overhand knot just above the beads and another tight knot to attach a jump ring. Carefully C&M the ends.

STEP 9 Open the ear hooks with pliers and cord them through the jump rings. Close them, and your macramé Diamond-Shaped Earrings are finished!

Owl Earrings

Macramé strands

Ten teal green, 20 inches (51 cm)

One teal-green holding cord the width of the board

Materials

Four 5-mm round wooden beads

Two 6-mm flat wooden beads

Twenty $2/3$-mm green glass beads

Two earring hooks

Six 4-mm metal jump rings

Knotting board + clips

Scissors

Pliers

Ruler & lighter

Inspired by the famous 1970s wall hanger macramé owl, these unique earrings hang beautifully thanks to the weight of the glass beads. They can easily be personalized by altering their length and color.

Dimensions: 2 inches (5 cm) long

Required Knots: Lark's head knot, square knot, diagonal double half hitch knot, overhand knot

STEP 1 Secure the teal green holding cord onto the board with two clips. Fold five strands in half and install using lark's head knots. This gives ten cords to work with.

STEPS 2 & 3 Separate the strands into three groups. Make a square knot using the first three cords on the left side. Repeat using the next four threads at the center, but do it with two holding cords inside the square knot. Then knot the last three strands on the right to finally get three square knots on the first row.

STEP 4 Leave one cord on each side and separate the other eight into two groups. Tie each group with a square knot to get two knots on the second row. Repeat with two holding cords inside each knot. To do the third row, tie a last square knot using the four cords in the middle.

STEP 5 Separate all the threads into two groups. Using the farthest right and farthest left cords as holding cords, make two diagonal lines with double half hitch knots going from the sides to the center. Do not join them together when they meet in the middle.

STEP 6 Pass both holding cords through the flat wooden bead and gently pull them taut. Keep the same holding cords to make the next two diagonal lines, but this time work from the center to the sides. Incorporate a round wooden bead onto one of the knotting cords.

STEP 7 Repeat Step 6 four more times to finally get five lines—each time take the first cord at the center as the holding cord. Repeat on both sides.

STEP 8 Make two successive big square knots with the last two holding cords, and use all the other strands as holding cords inside these knots. Make a second owl knotting by repeating all the steps.

STEP 9 Cut the holding cord on each side of the earrings, leaving a couple millimeters of threads for C&M. Repeat with the knotting cords used to make the last square knots.

STEP 10 Add one glass bead to each strand; secure with a simple overhand knot at the end. The position of the knot depends on how long you want the earrings. Cut the cords just under the knots and C&M.

STEP 11 Open two jump rings using pliers and pass them through the owl on each side of the center lark's head knot (made in Step #1). Close them. Take another jump ring, open it, and pass it through these two rings. Add the earring hook. Repeat this step with the other knotting. Your modern macramé Owl Earrings are finished.

Leaf Earrings

Macramé strands

Ten olive green, 23 inches (60 cm)

One holding cord the width of the board

Materials

Two 6-mm aventurine stone beads

Four 3-mm amethyst stone beads

Two 4-mm metal jump rings

Two earring hooks

Knotting board + clips

Scissors

Pliers

Ruler & lighter

Simple and perfect to wear every day! These leaf earrings are a perfect starter project for an introduction to macramé. This pair matches beautifully the Spring Leaves Pendant (page 38) if you want to create a set.

Dimensions: 2 inches (5 cm) long, including beads; the leaf measures 1.3 inches (3.5 cm)

Required Knots: Lark's head knot, diagonal double half hitch knot, overhand knot

STEP 1 Clip the holding cord horizontally. Fold five green strands in half and install them neatly using lark's head knots.

STEP 2 With your left hand, take the first right cord as the holding cord and knot double half hitch knots in a diagonal line. Work from right to left, knotting every other strand.

STEP 3 Leave the first strand on the right side and repeat Step 2, using the second cord as the holding cord. At the end of the second line, also knot the cord that was previously used as the holding cord.

STEP 4 Repeat Step 3 six more times, each time leaving the first strand on the right side. This makes eight shorter and shorter lines.

STEP 5 Take the holding cord used for the last line with your right hand and fold it back on itself. Tie double half hitch knots with the next two knotting cords.

STEP 6 Starting on the left side, take the first strand with your right hand and knot every cord used to create the previous line, but add one cord on the right. This will create the first small hole at the center of the leaf.

STEP 7 Repeat Step 6 six more times until the leaf is completed. Do not forget to add one more strand for each new line.

STEP 8 Make another leaf, repeating the same knotting. Once both leaves are done, pull off the holding cord. C&M all the cords that remain around each leaf except the holding cord used to make the last line. This is needed for the beads and to attach the earring hook.

STEP 9 Add the stone beads as shown below if you want to recreate the same pair, or be creative and choose a different combination. Tie an overhand knot just above the beads to secure them, then attach one jump ring on each earring with a second tight overhand knot. Carefully C&M the extremities.

STEP 10 Open the earring hooks with the pliers, pass them through the jump rings, and close. Do exactly the same with the second earring. Your bohemian Leaf Earrings are ready to wear!

Overlapping Squares Bracelet

Macramé strands
Ten teal blue, 98 inches (249 cm)
Three teal blue, 12 inches (30 cm)
One turquoise, 10 inches (25 cm)

Materials
Two 6-mm sodalite stone beads
Knotting board + clips
Scissors
Ruler & lighter

A very original bracelet pattern! This unusual wristband is composed of six overlapping macramé squares, which give an elaborate relief effect to the design.

Dimensions: 1 inch (2.5 cm) wide; 6 inches (15 cm) long

Required Knots: Lark's head knot, horizontal and vertical double half hitch knot, spiral square knot, overhand knot, three-strand braid

STEP 1 Secure the three 12-inch (30 cm) strands horizontally to the board. Fold the ten teal-blue strands in half. Install using lark's head knots, and separate them into two equal groups. The 12-inch (30 cm) strands will be used later to make the braids.

STEP 2 With the left-side group, make a horizontal line with double half hitch knots, working from left to right to the center point. Repeat with the right-side group, this time making a line from right to left. Join the two holding cords together with a double half hitch knot, then move them up and out of the way above the knotting—they are not used again in this first part of the pattern. Use a clip to block them at the top of the board.

STEP 3 Repeat Step 2 eight more times. Don't forget to leave and clip out of the way both holding cords after the lines are joined in the middle. A triangular shape with nine lines will start to form.

STEP 4 Separate the right and left strands into two groups with the same number of strands on each side. With the upper thread as the holding cord, make one vertical line of horizontal double half hitch knots with each group. You can turn the board around to make things easier.

STEP 5 Repeat Step 4 eight times on both sides until another triangular shape appears.

STEP 6 Separate the strands again into two equal groups. Use the farthest-left and farthest-right strands to make two horizontal lines. These will be joined in the middle.

STEP 7 The strands' positioning should now be in the same position as at the start. Repeat the steps over and again until there are six fully overlapping squares. Make two last vertical lines as before.

STEP 8 Work with the two vertical lines on the right. With your left hand, take the last knotting cord used to make the lines and knot it with vertical double half hitch knots, working from right to left around the two same holding cords. Then, with the same cord in your right hand, make vertical double half hitch knots coming back. Do the same on the left side, but reverse the direction of the knots.

STEP 9 Join together the two lines at the center. Then knot both sets of right and left cords together before joining them in the middle with a last double half hitch knot.

STEP 10 C&M all cords that remain in this part of the bracelet. Turn the macramé over and clip securely. Plait two 3½-inch (9 cm) three-strand braids and secure them with two overhand knots.

STEP 11 C&M two of the three threads above the knot braid. Incorporate the bead onto the third thread before making a last overhand knot.

STEP 12 Pass both braids through the hole you've created on the other side, and use the 10-inch (25 cm) turquoise strand to make a macramé sliding clasp with spiral square knots (page 10). Your Overlapping Squares Bracelet is done!

Three Squares Earrings

Macramé strands

Four navy blue, 20 inches (50 cm)

Four teal blue, 20 inches (50 cm)

Four turquoise, 20 inches (50 cm)

Four royal blue, 20 inches (50 cm)

Two white, 12 inches (30 cm)

One holding cord as long as the board width

Materials

Two 4-mm metal jump rings

Two earring hooks

Knotting board + clips

Scissors

Pliers

Ruler & lighter

These simple and fun square earrings will look great on anyone who likes blue. A perfect touch of color, they are a stylish addition to any summer outfit.

Dimensions: 2 inches (5 cm) long

Required Knots: Lark's head knot, diagonal double half hitch knot

STEP 1 Clip the holding cord to your board, and with lark's head knots, install two strands of each blue thread plus one white strand in the middle. Note that this knotting starts upside down. The big square will be made first, then the others.

STEP 2 For the rest of the project, only double half hitch knots are used. Knot both white strands together—using these two same threads as the holding cords, make two diagonal lines going out from the middle to both sides.

STEP 3 Next, work on the small teal-blue square inside the big square. Take the first royal-blue cord as the holding cord, and knot every teal-blue cord around it. Repeat this step with the next three royal-blue strands until the small teal-blue square is done.

STEP 4 For the royal-blue square, use the navy-blue threads as holding cords and the royal-blue ones as knotting cords. Perpendicular lines will form. Make four of them to get a small royal-blue square.

STEP 5 Make a turquoise square on the opposite side using the teal-blue strands as holding cords and the turquoise strands as the knotting cords. Finally, for the last small navy-blue square, take the turquoise strands as holding cords and knot every navy-blue strand onto them. Make two diagonal lines to finish the big square using the white cords as holding cords, and join them together when they meet in the middle with a last knot.

STEP 6 To make the medium square: Again using the white cords as holding cords, make two diagonal lines from the middle to both sides, but this time knot two strands of each blue instead of four. Leave the other strands; they are not needed again.

STEP 7 Make four small colored squares the same way as before. Finish the square with two diagonal lines, using the white cords as holding cords, and join them at the center.

STEP 8 Create a last very small square by repeating the same steps, but this time only use one strand of each blue for the first two diagonal lines.

STEP 9 Make a second earring by reversing the position of the blue strands from the very beginning. When both knots are done, pull off the holding cord, cut the remains of the strands, and carefully C&M the extremities to give a nice finish.

STEP 10 Open the jump rings using pliers and pass them through the knots, just under the last knot you made.

STEP 11 Add the earring hooks and jump rings to finalize your Three Squares Earrings.

Spring Leaves Pendant

Macramé strands

Three olive green, 39 inches (100 cm)

Seven olive green, 24 inches (60 cm)

Six lavender, 24 inches (60 cm)

Five light lime green, 24 inches (60 cm)

Four fuchsia pink, 20 inches (50 cm)

Three military green, 16 inches (40 cm)

Two beige, 12 inches (30 cm)

Materials

Four 6-mm amethyst stone beads

Four 3-mm aventurine stone beads

Knotting board + clips

Scissors

Ruler & lighter

This weightless pendant is perfect to wear in spring with this color combination—but feel free to be creative! You can choose any variation of colors to match your own wardrobe. Thanks to the macramé sliding clasp, you can adjust this pendant and wear it short or long.

Dimensions: Largest leaf 1¼ inches (3cm), smallest ¾ inch (3 cm); 3½ inches between stones

Required Knots: Lark's head knot, horizontal double half hitch knot, square knot, overhand knot, three-strand braid

STEP 1 Clip the three 39-inch (100 cm) olive-green strands horizontally across the board. Install all the other strands onto this foundation cord in the order shown in the photo—fold each strand in half, then tie in using reverse lark's head knots.

STEP 2 Start with the biggest leaf and work only on the olive-green strands on the left. Take the first olive-green cord on the right side with your left hand, and use it as the holding cord. Knot a horizontal line from right to left using double half hitch knots.

STEP 3 Repeat Step 2 seven more times, but each time you start a new line, leave the first thread on the right side. Remember to knot the previously used holding cord every time you finish a line. There should be eight increasingly shorter lines when this step is completed.

STEP 4 For the other half of the leaf: With your right hand, take the last cord used as a holding cord, fold it back on itself, and create a new line. Work from left to right, knotting the same six cords you just used to do the last line.

STEP 5 Return to the left side: Take the first olive-green strand with your right hand, and knot every cord used in Step 4 plus one cord up on the right side. This will create the first small hole at the center of the leaf.

STEP 6 Repeat Step 5 six more times until the leaf is completed. Remember to add one more strand for each line. When the first and the last threads join together, the first leaf is done!

STEP 7 Knot each of the other five leaves by repeating the steps. Use the next color cords each time. The only difference between leaves is the number of lines you have to make.

Knot eight lines in one direction and then in the other for the first three leaves—olive green, lavender, and light lime green. Knot six lines in one direction and then the other for the fuchsia pink, four lines for the military green, and three lines for the beige. When all the leaves are done, cut the cords that remain along the lower edge and underneath the knotting. C&M every extremity carefully to leave a neat finish.

STEP 8 Put a 6-mm bead in one of the three long strands, and make a square knot around it using the two other cords. Add a 3-mm bead and repeat using the same knot. Repeat on the other side.

STEP 9 Make two 12-inch (30 cm) three-strand braids. Secure them with an overhand knot at the end. Cut off two cords above each knot and C&M them, leaving just one cord on each side.

STEP 10 Incorporate a 6-mm stone bead followed by a 3-mm bead in each thread, and secure them with a last overhand knot.

STEP 11 Carefully and neatly C&M any excess ends.

STEP 12 Use an excess piece of thread to make a sliding clasp around the braids (page 12). Your Spring Leaves Pendant is finished!

Stone Beads & Diamond-Shaped Earrings

Macramé strands

Sixteen military green, 17½ inches (45 cm)

Two military green, 12 inches (30 cm)

Four orange, 14 inches (36 cm)

One holding cord as long as the board width

Materials

Four 6-mm carnelian stone beads

Four 3-mm amethyst stone beads

Two earring hooks

Knotting board + clips

Scissors

Pliers

Ruler & lighter

These stunning diamond-shaped macramé earrings are easily personalized to match your own taste. You can even create your own design here by incorporating as many dangling beads as you want at the end of the knotting.

Dimensions: Knotting is 1.3 inches (3.5 cm) long; earrings measure 2 inches (5 cm) including beads

Required Knots: Lark's head knot, diagonal and vertical double half hitch knot, square knot, overhand knot

STEP 1 Clip the holding cord horizontally to the board—the cord color does not matter. Fold one 12-inch (30 cm) military green strand in half and knot it with a lark's head knot. Place one orange strand on both sides using simple overhand knots, then four 17½-inch (45 cm) green cords with lark's head knots—four on both sides, as shown in the photo below.

STEP 2 Make a double half hitch knot with the two center green strands. Use these same two threads as the holding cords to make one diagonal line on each side with double half hitch knots.

STEP 3 On each side, use the orange thread as the knotting cord and knot vertical double half hitch knots to make two orange rows. At the end of the row, don't forget to also knot the green cords that were previously used as holding cords.

STEP 4 Take the two central green threads and knot them with a double half hitch knot. Use them as holding cords to make two more diagonal lines. Don't knot the orange strands when you get to the end of the lines.

STEP 5 Make a square knot using the four strands in the middle with two holding cords inside the knot. On the left side, make a second square knot (again with two strands inside) using the three next left strands. Add one of the knotting cords used previously to make the first square knot. Do the same on the right side. Finally make a fourth square knot in the middle with four strands.

STEP 6 Do one more square knot on the left with the next two green strands and one of the strands used in the last step; make this knot with only one strand inside the knot. Repeat on the right side.

STEP 7 Taking both cords coming out from the second square knot as holding cords, make another square knot with the two strands on each side. Repeat on the opposite side. Make a square knot in the middle with four strands.

STEP 8 Take the next left green thread **not** used for the square knots (i.e. the last one you knotted for the diagonal line above), and use it as the holding cord to do a line across to the center of your weaving. Repeat the step on the other side, and join both holding cords at the center with a double half hitch knot.

STEP 9 As before in Step 3, make vertical double half hitch knots with both orange strands, making one orange row on each side. Join them in the middle with a last double half hitch knot.

STEP 10 Finish the macramé square with two final diagonal green lines, using the furthest-right and furthest-left threads as the holding cords. Join them at the center.

STEP 11 Repeat every step to make a second earring. When both are done, remove the holding cord. On the lower part of the earring, C&M every thread except the last one used as the holding cord—this is needed to hold the beads. At the top of the earring, C&M every thread except the small center loop.

STEP 12 Incorporate the stone beads as shown—alternatively, be creative and personalize your creation however you like— and make a tight overhand knot to secure the beads.

STEP 13 Time to add the bead in the middle of the macramé square. Take one small strand from one of the offcuts, cord the bead onto it, and then pass both ends through the two small holes between the square knots in the center. Tie it on the back with two tight overhand knots, then C&M the cord above the knots.

STEP 14 To finish your Stone Beads & Diamond-Shaped Earrings, open the earring hooks with the pliers, pass them through the cord loops, and close them. That's it!

Amethyst & Squares Bracelet

Macramé strands

Eight olive green, 95 inches (241 cm)

Four olive green, 47 inches (120 cm)

One lavender, 10 inches (25 cm)

One holding strand as long as the board width

Materials

Two 3-mm amethyst stone beads

Two 6-mm amethyst stone beads

Knotting board + clips

Scissors

Ruler & lighter

With its pleasing simplicity, this bohemian style bracelet can be worn every day and will brighten up any outfit. It's very lightweight and readily adjustable. You'll never want to take it off!

Dimensions: Bracelet is 1.3 inches (3.5 cm) wide and 5.5 inches (14 cm) long

Required Knots: Lark's head knot, diagonal and vertical double half hitch knot, spiral square knot, overhand knot, three-strand braid

STEP 1 Clip the holding cord horizontally to the board—this thread is removed later. Install four 47-inch (120 cm) strands with simple overhand knots, leaving about 4 inches (10 cm) of the cords above the holding cord—these are used later to make a braid. On each side, add four 95-inch (241 cm) strands with lark's head knots, folding them in the middle.

STEP 2 Tie the two cords in the middle with a double half hitch knot. Use these same two strands as holding cords to make two diagonal lines going from the center to both sides with double half hitch knots.

STEP 3 Repeat Step 2 eight times to create nine lines on each side. Leave the holding cords at the end of each line—the lines will get shorter by themselves. A diamond shape will start to form.

STEP 4 To complete the diamond shape: Using the first lines as holding cords on both sides, make two diagonal lines running from the sides to the center. Join them together with a last double half hitch knot.

STEP 5 To create the curved side lines, the strands need to be woven in pairs. Start on the left side: Take the first-left cord and knot it around the second one, working from left to right with a vertical double half hitch knot. Then make a second knot using the same knotting cord, but this time do it from right to left. Continue making knots, reversing direction every time until there are ten of them—five in each direction.

STEP 6 In the same manner, make eight knots, then six knots, and finally four knots with the next cords.

STEP 7 After completing four curved lines, there will be two cords remaining on the left side. Use the right one as the holding cord, and make a long line going from right to left, tying every other strand with diagonal double half hitch knots.

STEP 7 (continued)
Continue knotting from right to left, tying every other strand with diagonal double half hitch knots.

STEP 8 Repeat Steps 5 and 7 on the right side, but reverse the direction of all the lines and knots—be careful about that!

STEP 9 Repeat Step 3 through Step 8 over and over to create four more diamond shapes.

STEP 10 When your knotting is complete, plait a 2-inch (5 cm) three-strand braid and secure it with an overhand knot at the end. Unclip the macramé and pull off the holding cord. Make a second braid as long as the first one using three of the four strands you installed with overhand knots in Step 1.

STEP 11 Neatly C&M all the remaining cord ends on both sides as well as two of the three cords above the braid's overhand knots. Cord the amethyst stone beads onto the third one before doing a last tight overhand knot. C&M.

STEP 12 To finish your Amethyst & Squares Bracelet, use the lavender thread to make a sliding clasp with spiral square knots (page 12).

Feathers & Turquoise Anklet

Macramé strands

Two dark brown, 32 inches (80 cm)

Two dark brown, 71 inches (180 cm)

One dark brown, 23$\frac{1}{2}$ inches (60 cm)

One dark brown, 75 inches (190 cm)

One holding cord as long as the board width

Materials

Twenty-six 3-mm turquoise stone beads

20 3-mm copper beads

Seven 2-cm copper feathers

Knotting board + clips

Scissors

Ruler & lighter

Note: If you want to make a pair of anklets, double the amount of strands and materials.

Inspired by Indian gypsy anklets, this is a perfect piece of jewelry to complete your bohemian summer outfit. This ankle bracelet with turquoise beads and copper feathers is great to wear barefoot or with leather sandals. If you want to make it longer, just cut longer macramé strands.

Dimensions: 7$\frac{1}{2}$ inches (19 cm) long

Required Knots: Lark's head knot, diagonal double half hitch knot, spiral square knot, overhand knot, three-strand braid

STEP 1 Set the holding cord with the clips. Install both 32-inch (80 cm) strands with overhand knots, leaving 6 inches (15 cm) of cord above the holding cord—these are used later to plait a braid. Then, on each side, install both 71-inch (180 cm) cords with lark's head knots, folding each of them in half.

STEP 2 Knot both centered cords together. Use these two same threads as holding cords to make one diagonal line on each side with double half hitch knots.

STEP 3 Take the left holding cord with your right hand and knot a diagonal line in the opposite direction using the same two strands—however, before knotting the second strand, thread a turquoise bead onto it. Repeat this step on the other side but without adding the bead. Join both holding threads together in the middle.

STEP 4 As before in Step 2, repeat two diagonal lines from the center out to both sides, but this time, before knotting the second-right strand, cord a copper bead onto it.

STEP 5 Repeat Steps 3 and 4, then Step 3 again, and then Step 4 again, but instead of adding a copper bead, add a copper feather through the second-right strand.

STEP 6 Repeat Step 3 through Step 5 over and over until there are seven attached feathers. After installing the last copper feather, keep doing the knotting to incorporate three more turquoise beads. This will make your anklet symmetrical.

STEP 7 For the left side spiral: Install the 23$\frac{1}{2}$-inch (60 cm) strand with an overhand knot, leaving 6 inches (15 cm) of strand above the holding cord. Take the 75-inch (190 cm) strand. Fold it in half and incorporate it onto the 23$\frac{1}{2}$-inch (60 cm) strand with a simple overhand knot (see next page).

STEP 8 Using the 23½-inch (60 cm) thread as the holding cord, tie repeated spiral square knots until the macramé spiral gets slightly longer than the right side knotting—about 0.4 inches (10 mm) longer.

STEP 9 Make a 4-inch (10 cm) three-strand braid with both the holding cords that were used in the first part of the project plus the spiral holding cord. Secure the braid with an overhand knot. Turn the anklet over and clip securely. Repeat this step with the three 6-inch (15 cm) strands left previously. When both braids are done, unclip the holding cord and pull it off. C&M every cord not used to make the braids.

STEP 10 At the end of the braids just above the last knot, C&M two of the three cords. Then incorporate two copper and one turquoise beads before doing a last overhand knot.

STEP 11 Use the holding cord you pulled off to do a macramé sliding clasp around the braids (page 12). Your Feathers & Turquoise Anklet is ready to wear!

Heart-Shaped Bracelet

Macramé strands

Two brownish orange, 79 inches (200 cm)

Four brownish orange, 71 inches (160 cm)

Four brownish orange, 36 inches (90 cm)

One brown, 10 inches (25 cm)

One holding cord (as long as the board width)

Materials

Two 3-mm tiger eye stone beads

Two 6-mm tiger eye stone beads

Knotting board + clips

Scissors

Ruler & lighter

This braided cuff designed with a succession of heart shapes is the perfect gift to offer someone you love. The fact that you made it with your own hands will make it even more special! Great to wear every day, it's lightweight and waterproof.

Dimensions: 1.2 inches (3 cm) wide and 5½ inches (14 cm) long

Required Knots: Lark's head knot, horizontal and vertical double half hitch knot, square knot, overhand knot, three-strand braid

Heart-Shaped Bracelet

STEP 1 Clip the holding cord horizontally to the board. Install all the 36-inch (90 cm) threads with simple overhand knots, leaving about 6 inches (15 cm) of thread above the holding cord. Then, on each side, fix two 71-inch (160 cm) and one 79-inch (200 cm) threads, folding them in half and making lark's head knots. This makes sixteen strands to work with.

STEP 2 Tie a double half hitch knot with the two central cords. Use these two same strands as holding cords to make one diagonal line on each side, working from the center to both sides.

STEP 3 Repeat the previous step, but at the end of the second line, remember to knot the previous holding threads.

STEP 4 Make a square knot in the middle with four strands (two holding cords inside the knot). Knot another on the right using two of the strands already used in the first square knot plus the next two righthand threads. Repeat on the left, and tie a last square knot in the middle. Finish with four knots in total.

STEP 5 On both sides, use the last holding cord to make one diagonal line going from the side to the center, and join both lines in the middle. Make another line on each side with the next-right and farthest-left strands. Join them at the center.

STEP 6 Make three square knots: Leave the two center cords, and make one knot on each side using the three next strands—this means using only one holding cord. Next, make another knot in the middle using the two unused central strands as holding cords.

STEP 7 Only two strands are used to make the curved sides for each line. Start on the left: Use the farthest-left strand as the knotting cord, and make one vertical double half hitch knot from left to right around the second thread. Reverse the knot direction, and make another vertical double half hitch knot with the same knotting cord. A shaped line will form. Repeat these knots until there are six double half hitch knots—three in each direction. Now take the two next threads and do four double knots in the same manner. On the right side, make two more curved lines, changing the knots' direction.

STEP 8 Join both shorter lines with the square knots' section: On the left side, take the shorter holding cord and knot every left-side square knot strand with horizontal double half hitch knots from left to right. Do the same on the other side, and join both lines at the center. Use the same technique to join the longer holding cords to the center part. Don't forget to join them in the middle of the knotting.

STEP 9 Repeat the last three steps nine more times to finally get ten heart shapes. If you want your bracelet to be longer, just make more heart shapes.

STEP 10 When the bracelet is long enough, use the three central strands to make a 2-inch (5 cm) three-strand braid, and secure it with an overhand knot at the end.

STEP 11 Pull off the holding thread. Unknot the four strands that were tied with overhand knots right at the beginning. Turn over the bracelet and clip securely, then make a second 2-inch (5 cm) three-strand braid.

STEP 12 C&M every remaining strand except those belonging to the braids' overhand knots. Incorporate the stone beads into the third strand of each braid, and make a last overhand knot. C&M.

STEP 13 Use the 10-inch (25 cm) brown strand to make a macramé sliding clasp around the braids (page 12). Your Heart-Shaped Bracelet is ready to wear . . . or give as a present!

Multicolor Camouflage Wristband

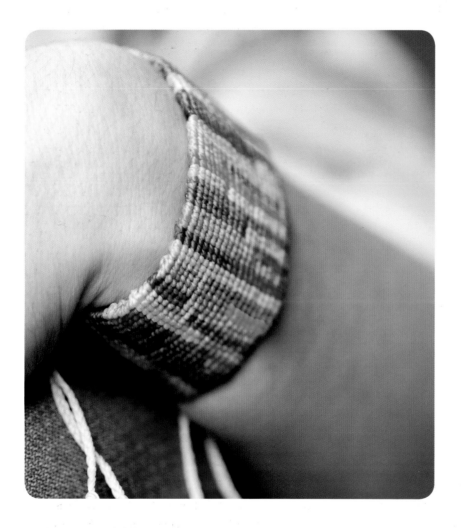

Macramé strands

Three white, 12 inches (30 cm)

Six white, 16 inches (40 cm)

Four white, 24 inches (60 cm)

Ninety mixed-color strands between 6 inches (15 cm) and 12 inches (30 cm)

Materials

Four 6-mm aventurine stone beads

Four 3-mm sodalite stone beads

Knotting board + clips

Scissors

Ruler & lighter

This bracelet is full of life with fun, vibrant colors in a camouflage design. It is perfect for a casual look and is also very beautiful in tones of a single color. The best thing about this project is that you can recycle leftover threads from other macramés.

Dimensions: 1.6 inches (4 cm) wide and 6 inches (15 cm) long

Required Knots: Lark's head knot, vertical and horizontal double half hitch knot, overhand knot, spiral square knot, three-strand braid

STEP 1 Clip three 12-inch (30 cm) white strands horizontally to the board. Install the six 16-inch (40 cm) strands and two 24-inch (60 cm) strands on each side with lark's head knots, folding them in half. This makes 20 threads to work with. The width can be easily modified by using more 16-inch (40 cm) white cords in the middle to make it wider or fewer to make it thinner.

STEP 2 Take one 12-inch (30 cm) color strand and knot it with a simple overhand knot onto the leftmost white thread. Then make a simple vertical half hitch knot on the same white strand to fix it.

STEP 3 Make a full colored row with vertical double half hitch knots, working from left to right and knotting each white strand until the row runs to the right side. Take an 8-inch (20 cm) color thread and install it on the rightmost white strand. Then knot it around the next seven white strands with vertical double half hitch knots, working from right to left.

STEP 4 Take a 10-inch (25 cm) color strand and place it on the ninth white thread as before. Knot it with vertical double half hitch knots across the width until you reach the last white thread on the left side.

STEP 5 Use the same color thread to tie three more vertical double half hitch knots, but this time work from left to right.

STEP 6 Take another 10-inch (25 cm) color thread and install it on the fourth white strand. Knot it with vertical double half hitch knots until it reaches the other side.

STEP 7 Continue repeating these last steps with various colored strands and sizes until the bracelet is the length needed. To make the colors appear random, vary the start and stop points.

STEP 8 Take the leftmost white thread as the holding cord and make a line with horizontal double half hitch knots to the center of the wristband. Repeat from the opposite side, starting with the rightmost white thread. Join both holding cords together at the center with a final knot.

STEP 9 Plait two 3-inch (8 cm) three-strand braids with the farthest-left and -right cords. Secure them with simple overhand knots. C&M two of the three threads above the knots and thread the stone beads onto the third one.

STEP 10 Flip the bracelet over and securely clip it. Repeat Step 9 with the three holding cords.

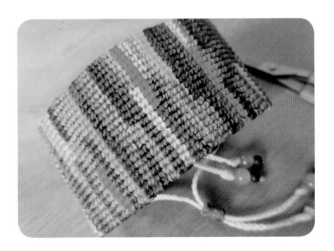

STEP 11 C&M all remaining threads. Make two macramé sliding clasps using spiral square knots (pages 10 and 12) around the braids to finalize your vibrant Multicolor Camouflage Wristband.

Winged Necklace

With shades of gray and blue, plus an impressive chrysocolla drop-shaped cabochon, this eye-catching, wing-shaped necklace is the perfect project to master every knot and technique taught in this book.

Macramé strands

Twenty-four gray, 67 inches (170 cm)

Eighteen gray, 8 inches (20 cm)

Nine gray, 12 inches (30 cm)

Eight gray, 16 inches (40 cm)

Eight gray, 20 inches (50 cm)

Two turquoise, 31 inches (80 cm)

Two sky blue, 31 inches (80 cm)

Two teal blue, 31 inches (80 cm)

Two navy blue, 31 inches (80 cm)

One turquoise, 10 inches (25 cm)

One gray strand at least 12 times the stone's perimeter, for wrapping the stone

Two gray strands at least 4 times the stone's perimeter, for wrapping the stone

Materials

One drop-shaped chrysocolla stone, 2 inches x 1.4 inch (50 mm x 35 mm)

Two 6 mm amazonite stone beads

Two 3 mm white quartz stone beads

Knotting board + clips

Needle & Scissors

Ruler & lighter

Dimensions: 7 inches (18cm) around the neckline; 2 inches (5cm) at the widest

Required Knots: Stone wrapping, horizontal and vertical double half hitch knot, lark's head knot, overhand knot, spiral square knot, three-strand braid

STEP 1 Wrap the chrysocolla stone with gray macramé knotting (pages 13–15). Join the wrapping at the base of the stone. (If the stone is smaller or larger, add more or fewer 8-inch [20 cm] strands as necessary in Step 3.) Using a needle, install a 12-inch (30 cm) gray strand, passing it through the wrapping at the top of the stone. Pull on it gently to center it.

STEP 2 Install twelve 67-inch (170 cm) strands on each side of the stone in the same way as before. Don't place them too close together. Once all twenty-four long strands are installed, they should surround three-quarters of the stone's perimeter.

STEP 3 Install ten 8-inch (20 cm) cords around the base of the stone—five on each side. The stone must be completely encircled. If it's not, simply add more strands.

STEP 4 Tie a horizontal double half hitch knot with the 12-inch (30 cm) strand at the top of the stone. Use these two same threads as holding cords to make two lines of horizontal double half hitch knots—one on the right-hand side and one on the left. Join both holding cords with a last double knot in the center.

STEP 5 Use the farthest-right and farthest-left 8-inch (20 cm) strands as holding cords. Make two small lines with double half hitch knots and join them in the middle. C&M every remaining 8-inch (20 cm) thread.

STEP 6 To work on the right side of the necklace, clip the left-hand threads up out of the way. Take the farthest-right cord as the holding cord. Make a line of knots, working from right to left until the last strand is reached. Repeat this step to make a second line. Don't forget to also knot the last holding cord at the end of the second line.

STEP 7 Take a 31-inch (80 cm) turquoise strand and knot it onto the rightmost strand with a simple overhand knot followed by a simple vertical half hitch knot; this fixes it in place. Working from right to left with vertical double half hitch knots, tie this turquoise cord around each gray strand until a complete blue row is knotted. But this time do not tie the last gray holding cord at the end.

STEP 8 Make another gray line as in Step 6. On completion, if things are done correctly, there should be twenty-two strands pointing toward you and three strands going off left—The turquoise thread between two gray threads.

STEP 9 In this next tricky part of the process you will work with the eight left strands pointing toward you. These are all holding cords, and every cord that is added becomes a knotting cord. Carefully examine the pictures and continually refer to them so the process will be easier to follow.

STEP 10 Take a 20-inch (50 cm) thread, fold it in half, and knot it onto the eighth strand with a reverse lark's head knot. Tie these two threads with double half hitch knots onto the seventh strand.

STEP 10 (continued) Knot around the sixth holding cord using one previous knotting cord. Add a 16-inch (40 cm) strand onto the same holding cord with a reverse lark's head knot before tying the second previous knotting cord.

STEP 10 (continued) On the fifth holding strand: Make double half hitch knots with all four threads. A triangular shape will start to form.

On the fourth strand: Tie two knotting threads with double half hitch knots and incorporate a 12-inch (30 cm) strand (the same way as before) before tying the two other knotting cords.

On the third strand: Knot every thread with double half hitch knots.

On the second holding cord: Tie three knotting cords before adding an 8-inch (20 cm) thread in the middle. Finish by tying the last three knotting cords.

Finally, on the leftmost holding cord: Tie every cord you've added here. This will make an eight-lined triangle.

STEP 11 Now work with the three long left-facing threads. Take the nearest gray thread and continue knotting with horizontal double half hitch knots all the way along the line. Tie every small thread that was added in the previous step plus every strand coming toward you. This line will go around the triangle and come back to where it started.

STEP 12 Continue knotting the turquoise-blue row with vertical double half hitch knots until you reach the fifteenth long gray strand pointing toward you. At this point, leave the turquoise thread underneath the project; it won't be needed anymore.

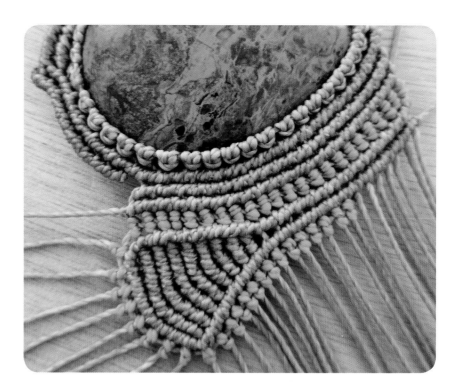

STEP 13 Take the last long thread going left: As before in Step 11, continue knotting the gray line until you reach the last right strand. At the end of this line, do not forget to also knot the last holding cord. Make this last line tight. The macramé knotting will curve, but this is absolutely fine.

STEP 14 Use the same last holding cord and make it come back from right to left to create another line. Continue until you reach the last long strand on the left side.

STEP 15 Repeat Step 7 through Step 14 three times using the 31-inch (80 cm) sky-blue thread, then the teal-blue thread, and finally the navy-blue thread.

STEP 16 Make ten lines: Work from right to left using the long threads, each time leaving the rightmost thread. Plait an 8-inch (20 cm) three-strand braid with the farthest left cords. Secure the braid with a simple overhand knot.

STEP 17 Repeat the same macramé knotting on the left side of the necklace. Remember to reverse the lines and the direction of the knots! When complete, C&M all remaining threads and two of the three threads above your braid's overhand knots. Thread the stone beads onto the left thread.

STEP 18 To finish the wing-shaped necklace, take a 10-inch (25 cm) turquoise thread and make a macramé sliding clasp with spiral square knots. (pages 10 and 12). Your stunning Winged Necklace is now complete and ready to wear out and about!

Red Jasper Stone Choker

Macramé strands

Twenty-two black, 36 inches (90 cm)

Fifteen black, 63 inches (160 cm)

Six black, 47 inches (120 cm)

One khaki, 36 inches (90 cm)

One khaki, 10 inches (25 cm)

Two black strands at least 12 times the stone's perimeter, for wrapping

Four strands at least 4 times the stone's perimeter, for wrapping

Materials

One oval red jasper stone, 1.8 x 1.2 inches (45 x 30 mm)

One oval red jasper stone, 1.3 x 0.9 inches (33 x 22 mm)

Sixteen 3-mm copper beads

Two 6-mm red jasper stone beads

Knotting board + clips

Needle

Scissors

Ruler & lighter

Note: In this project, it's essential to use stones of the stated size or be as close as possible to get the best result.

This dramatic black choker is definitely a statement piece with its two red jasper stones. Impressive and elegant at the same time, you'll want to wear it on the most special occasions!

Dimensions: 10½ inches (27 cm) around the neck; medallion, 4¾ inches (12 cm) long, by 4 inches (10 cm) wide, including stones

Required Knots: Stone wrapping, horizontal and vertical double half hitch knot, overhand knot, spiral square knot, three-strand braid

STEP 1 Wrap both stones with black macramé thread (pages 13–15). Complete the circle all the way around, then join and C&M the ends.

STEP 2 Start by working with the biggest stone. Using a needle, install one 36-inch (90 cm) black strand on the top of the stone, passing it through the wrapping and pulling gently until it is equally centered. Install another 36-inch (90 cm) thread under the first one.

STEP 3 In the same way, successively fix three 47-inch (120 cm) threads on both sides. Then fix ten 36-inch (90 cm) threads on each side until they join in the middle lower part of the stone. Don't put the cords too close together; leave a couple millimeters between them. When completed, there should be 56 cords to work with—these must cover the whole perimeter of the stone.

STEP 4 Make one horizontal double half hitch knot with the first strand installed at the top. Use these two same strands as holding cords to create two lines of horizontal double half hitch knots, one on each side of the stone. Join them when they meet in the middle of the stone with a last knot.

STEP 5 Swivel the knotting around to work on the back side so that the top part of the stone is in front of you.

STEP 5 (continued) Fix the 36-inch (90 cm) khaki thread with a simple overhand knot on the first left thread, plus one vertical half hitch knot on the same black cord. Then, doing vertical double half hitch knots from right to left, create a long khaki row all around the stone until you reach the last black thread.

STEP 6 Turn the piece around again to work on the front side. Using the first two black threads at the top of the stone, make two lines, one on each side, and join them in the middle of the lower part of the stone in the same way as with the first black line.

STEP 7 Clip the left-hand side cords to the top of your board, leaving room to work on the right side.

STEP 7 (continued) Separate a group of six threads at the center, leaving the eight farthest-left threads and the eight 36-inch (90 cm) threads on the right.

Use the first left cord of this group as the holding cord. Knot a line from left to right with horizontal double half hitch knots. Then make three increasingly shorter lines the same way, but leave the first left thread each time.

When half a leaf shape is knotted, fold the last holding cord so as to reverse back and work double half hitch knots from right to left with the next two cords—the same as with the last line.

STEP 8 To complete the leaf, make five more lines, incorporating the next left cord at the end of each line as shown in the photos above.

STEP 9 Use the first left thread at the bottom of the stone as the holding cord. Make a long line from left to right, knotting every other strand except the last holding thread you used for the leaf shape; just leave it underneath. Make five more lines the same way, starting with the second left strand (i.e., leaving the first left strand). Finally, complete the big leaf shape in the same way as the small one—knotting six lines in the opposite direction (from right to left) and adding one thread to each line.

STEP 10 Repeat the last three steps on the left side. Be careful here—do not forget to reverse the direction of the knots and lines! When it's done, join both last holding cords together with a final double half hitch knot.

STEP 11 Make two small leaves the same way you knotted the others—using six strands on each side and making four lines in one direction, followed by four return lines. Join both leaves with a last double half hitch knot as shown above. C&M the cords that remain around the bottom part of the stone and underneath the knotting.

STEP 12 Continue working on the right side of the necklace. Leave the five long strands on the right, instead working only with nine threads—eight short and one long. Use the first left thread as the holding cord, and knot a line from left to right. Then take the next left thread as the knotting cord, and make a black row by tying vertical double half hitch knots. At the end, do not forget to also knot the holding cord that was used for the first line. This knotting cord then becomes a holding cord— use it to knot a line from right to left with horizontal double half hitch knots and, as before, make a leaf shape with six lines in each direction.

STEP 13 Use the last holding cord to make the first line of a new leaf. Use six knotting cords and make five lines in each direction. When the leaf shape is complete, add one more similar line plus two shorter ones, using the third left thread as the holding cord.

STEP 14 Make two short lines, working from left to right with the five long strands at the top of the stone. Then take the leaf shape holding cord and tie the five threads with horizontal double half hitch knots to join both knottings.

Repeat these last three steps on the left side of the necklace, remembering to reverse the directions of all the knots and lines.

STEP 15 For the smaller stone: Using a needle, install one 63-inch (160 cm) thread on the center of the stone's top, plus seven more on each side—on completion, ¾ of the stone's perimeter will be surrounded with black strands.

On the right side of the stone: Using the first left cord as a holding cord, knot a line until you reach the center of the stone's top. Repeat on the left side of the stone using the first right cord. Tie both holding cords together with a last knot where they meet at the top.

Now join both stones together. Knot the big stone's two last holding cords on each side of the upper stone. Now they become knotting cords. Tie these two strands with vertical half hitch knots and join them where they meet at the top of the stone. Use the big stone's second strands as holding cords to make one line on each side with horizontal double half hitch knots. Join them together where they meet at the top of the small stone.

STEP 16 Work on the right side of the small stone. Using the leftmost strand as a holding cord, make a line almost to the top, just leaving the two last threads. Use the same holding cord to make another line, but this time from right to left and tying only six knotting cords. Then, with the eight leftmost threads, make a left-to-right line until you reach the previous one and join them.

STEP 17 Separate the cords into two groups with eight strands on the left and seven strands on the right. With the left group: Starting from the left, take the fifth thread and knot it around the three right cords with vertical double half hitch knots. Repeat with the fourth thread. Thread three copper beads onto the third thread and repeat the knotting. Repeat this step with the right group, reversing the direction of the knots and lines. Close the central line eye-shape by tying back the same threads onto the same holding cord—to do this, reverse the order of the diagonal direction and the knotting cords. Join both lines in the middle. Repeat with the second and third holding threads to complete the three lines eye-shape. Make a second similar eye-shape without copper beads. Use the three outermost strands as knotting cords.

STEP 18 Make two smaller eye shapes using just two holding cords and two knotting cords. Repeat, making two smaller ones with one holding cord and two knotting cords. Finally, make two even smaller shapes using only one holding cord and one knotting cord.

Step 19 Tie a few spiral square knots (page 10). C&M one thread on the side and make an 8-inch (20 cm) braid with the others. Secure it with a simple overhand knot.

Step 20 Weave the left side of the necklace: Return to Step 16, but reverse every line and knot direction. Be very careful here—right becomes left and vice versa!

Step 21 After knotting the second braid, C&M two of the three cords above the overhand knots and incorporate the stone/copper beads onto the third cord before completing with a last overhand knot. Neatly C&M all the threads remaining around the necklace.

Step 22 Use a 10-inch (25 cm) khaki strand to make a macramé sliding clasp (page 12), and your Red Jasper Stone Choker is ready to wear!

Black & Brown Gradient Wristband

Macramé strands

Twenty-six black, 39 inches (100 cm)

Eight orange, 12 inches (30 cm)

Eight caramel brown, 12 inches (30 cm)

Eight gold brown, 12 inches (30 cm)

Eight dark brown, 12 inches (30 cm)

One orange, 10-inch (25 cm)

One black strand at least 12 times the stone's perimeter, for wrapping

Two black strands at least 4 times the stone's perimeter, for wrapping

Materials

One round tiger's eye stone, 1.2 x 1.2 inches (30 mm x 30 mm)

Two tiger's eye stone beads 0.11-inch (3 mm)

Two tiger's eye stone beads 0.23-inch (6 mm)

Knotting board + clips

Needle

Scissors

Ruler & lighter

Humorously named the "Inca's clock" by my Peruvian macramé teachers and friends because of its shape, this elegant black bracelet can be worn as an original armlet. Depending on your wrist or arm size, you can easily make it longer or smaller by adding more or fewer brown lines during the knotting process.

Dimensions: 2.2 inches (5.5 cm) wide and 6 inches (15 cm) long

Required Knots: Stone wrapping, horizontal and vertical double half hitch knot, overhand knot, spiral square knot, three-strand braid

Note: For this project, try to use a cabochon stone of the diameter stated or as close as possible.

STEP 1 Wrap the stone with black macramé knotting (pages 13–15).

Using a needle, install two black strands—one at the top and one at the bottom of the stone—passing them through the wrapping and gently pulling them so they are equally centered.

STEP 2 Install 12 black strands on each side of the stone the same way as before. Once all 26 strands are installed, they should surround the entire stone perimeter.

STEP 3 Knot the first top strand with a double half hitch knot. Use these same two threads as holding cords to make one line on each side with the next 12 knotting cords. Repeat, starting with the first strand installed at the bottom of the stone. Join the holding cords together when they meet on the side.

STEP 4 Before starting to knot the right side, clip all the lefthand threads out of the way at the top of the board. Check that there are twenty-six threads on each side before starting to knot. Use the farthest-left and farthest-right threads as holding cords, and make two lines with horizontal double half hitch knots, one on each side. Join them together with a last knot at the center.

STEP 5 Take one 12-inch (30 cm) orange strand and incorporate it on the first right strand with a simple overhand knot plus a simple vertical half hitch knot around the same black thread. Working from right to left, tie this orange thread with vertical double half hitch knots around each black thread until you reach the middle of the bracelet. Do the same on the left side, reversing the direction of the knots. Join both orange strands with a last knot at the center.

STEP 6 Use the extreme-left and -right cords as holding cords. Make two black lines as before. Do not knot the orange strands at the ends of the row; leave them underneath your knotting before joining the holding cords.

STEP 7 Repeat Steps 5 and 6 seven times, using a different color each time. If you want the bracelet to be longer or shorter, you can add or reduce rows.

STEP 9 Turn the bracelet around and work on the left side. Repeat every step from Step 4 onwards. When complete, C&M all remaining threads.

STEP 10 To finish the Black & Brown Gradient Wristband, make a macramé sliding clasp (page 12) around the braids with a 10-inch (25 cm) orange thread.

STEP 8 Plait a 2-inch (5 cm) three-strand braid with the central cords, and secure the braid with a simple overhand knot. C&M two of the three threads above the knot, and thread the stone beads onto the third thread.

White & Blue Necklace

Macramé strands

Three white, 75 inches (190 cm)

Two teal, 75 inches (190 cm)

Two royal blue, 75 inches (190 cm)

Two turquoise, 75 inches (190 cm)

One light sky blue, 75 inches (190 cm)

One light sky blue, 10 inches (25 cm)

One white strand at least 12 times the stone's perimeter, for wrapping

Two white strands at least 4 times the stone's perimeter, for wrapping

Materials

1 turquoise stone, 1.8 x 1 inch (45 mm x 25 mm)

Two white quartz stone beads 0.23-inch (6 mm)

Two lapis lazuli stone beads 0.11-inch (3 mm)

Knotting board + clips

Needle

Scissors

Ruler & lighter

This lovely necklace gets its color inspiration from the deep blue sea and the white-and-blue villages of Greece, which is the perfect spot to wear this kind of piece! The good thing about this project is that the medallion size and shape are not crucial for the success of the necklace—you are free to make this necklace with any size and shape of stone, provided you can wrap it!

Dimensions 10½ inches (27 cm) around the neckline; medallion 4 inches (10 cm) wide and 4¾ inches (12 cm) long, including stones

Required Knots: Stone wrapping, horizontal and vertical double half hitch knot, overhand knot, spiral square knot, three-strand braid

STEP 1 Wrap the stone with white macramé knotting (pages 13–15). Join the knotting at the top of the stone. Using a needle, install a 75-inch (190 cm) white strand, passing it through the wrapping at the top of the stone and pulling gently so it is equally centered. Install the two other white threads on either side in the same way.

STEP 2 Use the farthest-left thread as the holding cord. Tie the next two cords with double half hitch knots, working from left to right. Repeat with the farthest-right thread, working from right to left. Join both holding cords together.

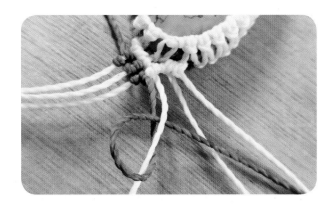

STEP 3 Take a teal strand and make a simple overhand knot right in the middle before passing it through the third white thread. Tighten the ends and then push it up against the white lines before making a simple vertical half hitch knot around the same white thread. Make sure the blue thread length is the same on each side. Around each white thread, tie vertical double half hitch knots, working from right to left with the left-side blue, then from left to right with the right-side blue.

STEP 4 Repeat Step 3 six times using another teal strand, then two royal-blue, two turquoise, and finally one light sky-blue strand.

STEP 5 Knot the two center white strands together with a horizontal double half hitch knot using the left thread as the holding cord. This thread then becomes a knotting cord, which you must knot around the next white thread on the right side. Do the same the opposite way, knotting two threads on the second left cord. Finally, use the first right white thread and knot the two next threads. Do the same on the opposite side with three knotting threads.

STEP 6 Clip all the lefthand strands at the top of your knotting board so you can work on the right side of the necklace. Make seven lines from right to left with horizontal double half hitch knots, each time leaving the first thread on the right.

STEP 7 Make the last holding cord return in the opposite direction. Knot both next knotting cords with horizontal double half hitch knots, but this time work from left to right. Make a second line using the left-most thread, but add one more knotting cord on the right. Repeat, doing lines the same way until you have seven of them. At the end of the last line, add two threads on the right instead of only one.

STEP 8 Knot the two farthest-right threads together with a double half hitch knot, using the second strand as the knotting cord. Repeat this knot three more times until you have four knots in total. Alternate the holding and knotting cords each time. Similarly, make three knots with the next two threads, two knots with the following two threads, and one knot with the royal-blue thread. Still using double half hitch knots, use the last holding cord to make a line from right to left. Repeat twice more.

STEP 9 Repeat Step 8 again, but this time start the four knots with the farthest-left threads.

STEP 10 Continue knotting the wavy lines as before. Repeat once, starting with both right threads, and then twice more, starting with the farthest-left threads.

STEP 11 Turn the last holding cord to come back on itself, and use it to make a line from right to left. Then make 11 similar lines, each time using the farthest-right thread as the holding cord.

STEP 12 Plait an 8-inch (20 cm) three-strand braid with the strands on the left, and secure it with an overhand knot. C&M two of the three threads above the knot, and thread the stone beads onto the third cord.

STEP 13 Weave the left side of the necklace, repeating Step 6 through Step 12, reversing the direction of the lines and knots.

STEP 14 C&M all remaining threads. Use a 10-inch (25 cm) light sky-blue cord to create a macramé sliding clasp with spiral square knots (pages 10 and 12) around the braids.

Fall Leaves Necklace

Macramé strands

Seventy-six brownish orange, 20 inches (50 cm)

Four brownish orange, 32 inches (80 cm)

Forty military green, 20 inches (50 cm)

Forty-eight apple green, 20 inches (50 cm)

Twenty-four regular green, 20 inches (50 cm)

Four bright orange, 20 inches (50 cm)

Eighteen beige, 16 inches (40 cm)

One bright orange, 10 inches (25 cm)

One bright-orange strand at least 12 times the stone's perimeter, for wrapping

Two bright-orange strands at least 4 times the stone's perimeter, for wrapping

One holding cord as long as the board width

Materials

One oval malachite stone, 2.2 x 1.4 inches (55 x 35 mm)

Two 6-mm red jasper stone beads

Two 3-mm carnelian stone beads

Knotting board + clips

Needle

Scissors

Ruler & lighter

This statement necklace made in fall tones is spectacular, with a great relief effect on the leaves. It's not as difficult to knot as it looks, although it will take patience—but the result is well worth it. Be creative with this project by choosing your own color combinations or other seasonal colors. You can use a different main stone size or shape and still follow the steps without creating problems. Depending on your patience, you are free to make as many leaves for this necklace as you like!

Dimensions: 6³/₄ inches (17 cm) across the neckline; 2³/₄ inches (17cm) at the widest

Required Knots: Stone wrapping, horizontal double half hitch knot, lark's head knot, overhand knot, spiral square knot, and three-strand braid

STEP 1 Wrap your stone with bright-orange macramé knotting (pages 13–15). Join the wrapping. C&M the excess thread.

STEP 2 Leave a 1-inch (2.5 cm) gap at the top of the stone. With a needle, install four 20-inch (50 cm) bright-orange, four apple-green, and four regular-green strands on the left side. Do the same on the right side, with regular-green first, then brownish-orange, and finally apple green.

STEP 3 Clip all the right-hand cords out of the way at the top of the board. For the bright-orange strands: Create a leaf shape by knotting horizontal half hitch knots and working from right to left in six increasingly shorter lines. Use the first right cord as the holding thread; knot the first line from right to left. Repeat with the next five strands, each time leaving the right-side cord, and then successively using the second thread as the holding cord.

STEP 4 To complete the leaf: Take the holding cord back on itself with your right hand, then knot again using the same two threads, but this time work from left to right. Knot another line using the farthest-left thread as the holding cord. At the end, add one more knotting cord on the right. Repeat, making lines the same way until the leaf shape is complete.

STEP 5 Repeat Steps 3 and 4 with the apple-green threads. Make a third leaf shape with the regular-green thread, starting by knotting lines from left to right so that the leaf shape points downwards.

STEP 6 Make three more leaf shapes on the right side: one pointing up, starting with lines working from left to right, and two pointing down, starting with lines from right to left. On completion, C&M all the threads that remain on the sides.

STEP 7 Patience is needed for this stage as each leaf needs to be made separately. To make exactly the same necklace as shown here, knot 48 individual leaves. To be precise, knot 18 brownish-orange, ten apple-green, ten military-green, and four regular-green leaves. Then, finally, using only three strands instead of four, make six smaller beige leaves.

To knot the leaves—remember, this must be done one at a time—working from right to left, clip the holding cord to your board and install four strands with lark's head knots for each leaf. Use three strands for the smaller leaves. Use the same technique as before with the leaves around the stone, but instead of doing horizontal lines, start off with six diagonal lines in one direction and six in the opposite direction to complete the knotting. Refer to the Leaf Earrings project (page 24) for detailed pictures. When you C&M the threads, keep all the longest threads; they will be useful when joining all the leaves together.

STEP 8 Once all the leaves are knotted—but before joining them—arrange the leaves next to each other to balance out the colors and spacing. It helps to take a photograph as a reference; this will make things a lot easier when you are in the process of joining every leaf.

STEP 9 Each leaf needs two secured points hidden away under the previous leaves. To join a brownish-orange leaf under a bright-orange leaf and an apple-green leaf, you will need to use one bright-orange and one apple-green thread from your excess thread. Thread a suitable needle with the excess, and pass it through both weavings—one way from underneath and then back again from the top. Make a tight overhand knot underneath the leaf where it won't be seen. C&M above each knot to complete.

STEP 10 Once all the leaves are joined together, it is time to add the threads for the braids. Pass two 32-inch (80 cm) brownish-orange strands through the last leaf hole and make a few spiral square knots before weaving an 8-inch (20 cm) four-strand braid. Secure this with a simple overhand knot, and plait it as if it were a three-strand braid. Do the same on the other side. C&M three of the four threads above the knots. Incorporate the stone beads onto the last one.

STEP 11 Use the 10-inch (25 cm) bright-orange thread to make a sliding clasp around the braids (page 12). Your impressive Fall Leaves Necklace is ready to wear!

Amethyst & Copper Anklet

Macramé strands

Three military green, 47 inches (120 cm)

Six military green, 78 inches (200 cm)

Sixteen military green, 26 inches (70 cm)

Two lavender, 13 inches (35 cm)

One lavender, 10 inches (25 cm)

Two eggplant, 13 inches (35 cm)

Two eggplant, 6 inches (15 cm)

Two khaki, 6 inches (15 cm)

Materials

Two 8-mm amethyst stone beads

Five 6-mm amethyst stone beads

Eight 3-mm amethyst stone beads

Twenty-five 3-mm copper beads

Knotting board + clips

Scissors

Ruler & lighter

Glam up your feet with this stylish anklet that looks like a sandal. It's perfect to wear barefoot on the beach or at home for great bohemian style. You can adjust the length for your foot size in the last steps.

Note: To make a pair of anklets, double the amount of thread and beads.

Dimensions: about 5 inches (13 cm) long from the top center to the ring

Required Knots: Lark's head knot, horizontal and vertical double half hitch knot, overhand knot, spiral square knot, three-strand braid

STEP 1 Clip the three 47-inch (120 cm) green strands horizontally to your board, and install ten 26-inch (70 cm) threads. Fold them in half and install with reverse lark's head knots, but be sure to place them at the center of the 47-inch (120 cm) cords. Then, on both sides, fold in half and successively add one 78-inch (200 cm) strand, three more 26-inch (70 cm) strands, and finally, two 78-inch (200 cm) strands. This gives you 44 threads to work with. Now attach the original 47-inch (120 cm) threads with two clips at the top of the board to form a "U" shape. Separate them into two equal groups of 22 threads.

STEP 2 Use the farthest-left and farthest-right threads as holding cords. Make one line on each side with horizontal double half hitch knots. Join both holding cords with a last knot where they meet in the middle. Repeat this step a second time to get two lines on each side. When this is done, clip the last two holding cords out of the way at the top of the board; they will be needed later.

STEP 3 In the same way make three more lines on either side, but before knotting each line, thread a 3-mm amethyst bead onto the second strand (i.e. the first actual knotting cord). But don't join the end of each line with the opposite side like you did in the previous step.

STEP 4 Turn over the knotting to work on the back. Take a 13-inch (35 cm) lavender thread and incorporate it onto the first right strand with a simple overhand knot. Add a simple vertical half hitch knot around the same green thread. Knot this lavender cord using vertical double half hitch knots around each green thread, working from right to left until you reach the end of the line. Do the same on the left side, reversing the direction of the knots. Return to the front and make another green line on each side like before.

STEP 5 Repeat the previous step with two 13-inch (35 cm) eggplant threads.

STEP 6 Go back to the two green threads that you clipped away in Step 2. Use these as holding cords to make two perpendicular lines. To achieve this, knot the five holding cords used for the last green lines on each side—do not tie the lavender and eggplant cords! Leave them out of the way underneath the weaving.

STEP 7 To complete the eye shape, knot back every cord on the same holding cords but reverse the direction of the diagonal and the knotting cord order. Incorporate one 8-mm amethyst bead between two copper beads in the last knotting cord before joining both lines in the middle.

STEP 8 All the eye-shape cords will now become knotting cords. Knot them around the closest left and closest right strands to make one more line on each side. Join them in the middle with a last double half hitch knot. Repeat this step to finish with three lines.

STEP 9 For the 14 left-side strands: Leave the first two on the left and knot the others two-by-two, working from left to right, making only one vertical double half hitch knot. Then use the first holding cord to make a long diagonal line with double half hitch knots. Continue knotting this line, joining the eye-shape cords in the process. Do the same on the right side, reversing the directions.

STEP 10 After both long lines have joined, incorporate one copper bead by passing it through both cords. Use these same threads as holding cords to again make two diagonal lines with four knotting cords on each side. Before knotting the fourth strand, thread on six copper beads. Now complete the second eye-shape, knotting back these same threads and adding another 8-mm amethyst bead.

STEP 11 Make a second green line after the eye-shape with the farthest-left and-right cords. Turn over the weaving to add a khaki row (as previously with the lavender and eggplant). Return to the front. Knot another green line, but on reaching the holding cords in the middle, do not knot the khaki threads; leave them alone, tucked underneath. Make another eggplant row on the back and two others in green lines on the front. After completing the first of these two green lines, leave the first thread on both sides.

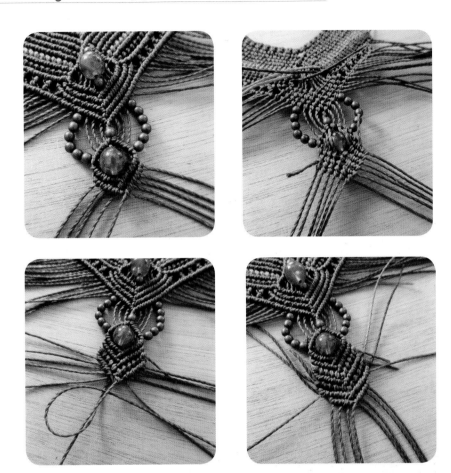

STEP 12 Use the two center threads as holding cords to make a diagonal line on each side. Incorporate one copper bead onto the second knotting cords and two copper beads onto the third ones. Then close the eye-shape, making two more diagonals and adding one 6-mm amethyst bead.

109

STEP 13 Make four more lines on each side, using the furthest-left and furthest-right cords successively plus three lines, but leave the first strands on each line alone. In this step, you can do more or fewer lines to modify the length of your creation.

STEP 14 Using the two left threads, incorporate a copper bead onto the first strand. Make a vertical double half hitch knot from left to right with the second one. Change hands and make a second knot with the same thread, working from right to left

STEP 15 Repeat vertical knots over and over to make a row of knots at least 2 inches (5 cm) long, but be careful here; depending on your foot size, you may need to make it longer or shorter. C&M the knotting cord. Add one copper bead before creating a ring by doing a final, very tight double half hitch knot with the first right thread.

STEP 16 Clip the weaving upside down to work with the 47-inch (120 cm) strands. Choose a side, incorporate one 6-mm amethyst bead on one thread, and make ten spiral square knots with the two others just over the bead. Plait a 14-inch (35 cm) braid—or longer depending on your ankle size—and secure it with a simple overhand knot at the end. C&M two of the three cords above the knot before adding the three beads. Repeat this step to make the second braid. Use a 10-inch (25 cm) lavender strand to make a macramé sliding clasp (page 12).

To make a pair of anklets, repeat the entire process again.

Three Stones Wristband

Macramé strands

Fourteen dark red, 47 inches (120 cm)

Four dark red, 24 inches (60 cm)

Ten dark red, 16 inches (40 cm)

Six bright red, 47 inches (120 cm)

Twelve brown, 47 inches (120 cm)

Eight military green, 47 inches (120 cm)

Four orange, 8 inches (20 cm)

Two orange, 10 inches (25 cm)

Three orange strands at least 12 times the stone's perimeter, for wrapping

Six strands at least 4 times the stone's perimeter, for wrapping

Materials

One oval-shaped tiger's eye stone, 30 mm x 20 mm

Two oval-shaped tiger's eye stones, 25 mm x 15 mm

Four 3-mm tiger eye stone beads

Four 6-mm tiger eye stone beads

Knotting board + clips

Needle

Scissors

Ruler & lighter

This unique macramé creation is inspired by wonderful, wide Indian wristbands, but it is made with knots instead of silver. Very eyecatching with its three tiger eye gemstones, this piece has an undeniably powerful energy! It's also very striking if you wear it up around your forearm.

Dimensions: 5 inches (12 cm) wide, made for a 6-inch (15 cm) wrist

Required Knots: Stone wrapping, horizontal and vertical double half hitch knot, overhand knot, spiral square knot, three-strand braid

STEP 1 Wrap each stone with orange macramé knotting (pages 13–15). In this project, it's important to use stones of the stated size in the supply list, or try to find stones as close in size as possible to get the best result. When installing the cords in the next step, be careful to place them symmetrically so that they cover the stone's whole perimeter.

STEP 2 Start with the center stone, the largest one. With a needle, install two 47-inch (120 cm) dark-red strands. Pass them through the wrapping—one at the top of the stone and one at the bottom. Next, on both sides of these threads install one 24-inch (60 cm) dark-red, two 47-inch (120 cm) brown, one 47-inch (120 cm) dark-red, one military-green, and finally one bright-red strand in exactly the middle of the sides—24 cords in total, which will give you forty-eight threads to work with.

STEP 3 Make one horizontal double half hitch knot with the first strand. Use these same two threads as holding cords to make one line on each side. Make horizontal double knots along the lines and tie every thread until you reach the first bright-red cord in the middle. Do the same on the opposite side. Join the holding cords together with a last double knot.

STEP 4 Now let's install the thread around the side stones. As for each stone before, install one 16-inch (40 cm) dark-red strand on the side that will be joined with the center stone. Install on both sides of this cord one 47-inch (120 cm) bright-red, two 47-inch (120 cm) dark-red, one military-green, one brown, and finally two 16-inch (40 cm) dark-red strands. This gives you 15 strands evenly spaced on each stone to cover the whole perimeter. Make one horizontal double half hitch knot with the first strand you placed (on the side that will be joined with the center stone) and then use these two threads as holding cords to make one line on each side. These will be joined when they meet on the opposite side.

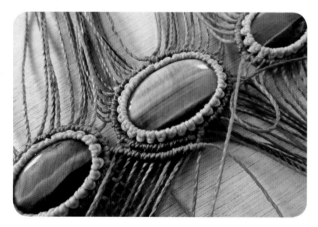
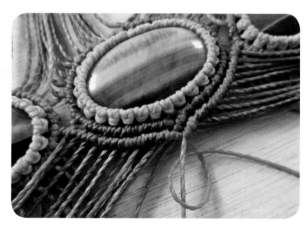

STEP 5 The stones are now ready to be joined. Place the three stones as shown in the photos above. Knot the center stone cords with horizontal double half hitch knots around the first bright-red cords coming from the side stones. This will create one line on each side. Then join both bright-red cords in the middle. Repeat this step on the other side of the wristband to complete the joining.

STEP 6 To weave one side of the wristband: Select the section you want to work on and clip the other side cords away at the top of the board. Use the second bright-red strand on the side to make a long red row with vertical double half hitch knots until you reach the center.

STEP 7 Repeat Step 6 on the other side and join both knotting cords where they meet in the middle.

STEP 8 Use the next three dark-red threads on the sides as holding cords to make three lines with horizontal double half hitch knots.

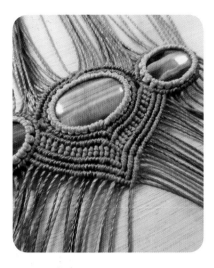

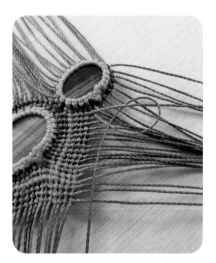

STEP 8 (continued) Each time you finish a line, join the holding cords at the center.

STEP 9 Turn over the knotting to work on the back. Make vertical double half hitch knots with the next dark-red strand coming off the side stone. Do this on both sides, and join both dark-red rows in the middle.

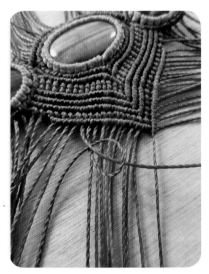

STEP 10 Make two lines, one on each side, using the dark-red cords (the one just after the green strands) as holding cords. Join them in the middle with a last double knot.

STEP 10 (continued) Taking the farthest-left and farthest-right green strands, make vertical double half hitch knots to make a green row on each side. Join them at the center. Finally, make two more lines on each side with the next two farthest-right and farthest-left cords.

STEP 11 Repeat the same macramé knotting on the other side of the wristband.

STEP 12 Now, to knot around the side stones, choose one side and clip the other side cords out of the way at the top of the board. Use the first dark-red thread as the holding cord (one of the two cords left previously on the central part of the wristband) to make a line. Do this on both sides, and join the two holding cords together at the top of the stone.

STEP 13 Work on the back. Take one 8-inch (20 cm) orange thread and incorporate it on the farthest-right dark-red cord with a simple overhand knot plus one vertical half knot. Then make double vertical half hitch knots until you reach the middle. Repeat on the other side and join both orange lines where they meet. Return to the front. Make one line on each side with the farthest-left and farthest-right cords. Join them at the center.

STEP 12 (continued) Repeat one line on each side with the second dark-red thread to ultimately get three lines around the stone.

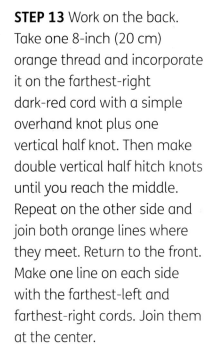

STEP 14 Repeat Steps 12 and 13 with the other side stone. C&M the threads you used to do the last line. Be careful not to cut the brown and green threads; you'll need them in the next step.

STEP 15 Clip the macramé knotting to work on the back. Use the brown and green four-strand group on the right (see the last two pictures, bottom right, on page 118). Make three small lines of horizontal double half hitch knots, working from left to right, and each time using the farthest-left thread as the holding cord. On the second and third line, be sure you also knot the previous holding cord at the end.

Fold this same holding cord back on itself to make a line from right to left. Make nine other lines using the farthest-right threads as holding cords. Again, be sure to always knot the previous holding cord at the end of each line. On the tenth line knotting, add the center cords with the same horizontal double half hitch.

Repeat this entire step on the other side of the piece, but reverse the line directions. Join both last holding cords when they meet in the middle.

STEP 16 On the front: Using the farthest-left and farthest-right cords in turn as the holding cords, make three lines on each side with horizontal double half hitch knots. Join them in the middle every time you finish a line.

STEP 17 On the back: Repeat Step 15 with the four-strands group you previously left. This time, make seven lines one way and five lines in the opposite direction. Remember to continue knotting the last line until the center point. Do this on both sides and join them in the middle.

STEP 18 On the front: Make two last long lines on each side with the farthest-left and farthest-right cords, and join them at the center.

STEP 19 With the left side strands: Make six lines from left to right until you reach the first green cord. In this case, you don't have to knot the previous holding cord when you finish a line—that's why the lines become shorter and shorter all by themselves. Use the second green strand as the holding cord to make a perpendicular line. The six holding cords now become knotting cords. When this line is done, plait a 2.4-inch (6 cm) three-strand braid and secure it with an overhand knot. Repeat this step on the right side, reversing the direction of the lines.

STEP 20 Repeat the exact same macramé knotting on the other side of your wristband.

STEP 21 C&M all the threads that remain, and two of the three strands above the braids knot. Incorporate the stone beads onto the third cord and secure them with a simple tight knot.

STEP 22 To finish your Three Stones Wristband, use two 10-inch (25 cm) orange threads to create two sliding clasps around the braids (page 12).

Stone Fringes Necklace

Macramé strands

Three brown, 39 inches (100 cm)

Twenty-four brown, 19 inches (50 cm)

Six brown, 28 inches (70 cm)

Eight navy blue, 16 inches (40 cm)

Two turquoise, 18 inches (45 cm)

One turquoise, 10 inches (25 cm)

Materials

27 $2/3$-mm turquoise stone beads

82 $2/3$-mm lapis lazuli stone beads

29 $2/3$-mm copper beads

Knotting board + clips

Scissors

Ruler & lighter

This brown breastplate necklace with its lapis lazuli, turquoise, and copper bead fringes evokes some exotic piece of African jewelry and alludes to the origins of macramé, a word derived from the Arabic *migramah*, which means "ornamental fringe."

Dimensions: 2.4 inches (6 cm) from the central top point of the macramé to the last bead in the middle of the fringe; 4.3 inches (11 cm) between both sides

Required Knots: Lark's head knot, horizontal and vertical double half hitch knot, overhand knot, spiral square knot, three-strand braid

STEP 1 Clip the 39-inch (100 cm) threads horizontally across the board. Using lark's head knots, install the twenty-four 19-inch (50 cm) brown cords. Then, on either side, add three 16-inch (40 cm) navy- blue and three 28-inch (70 cm) brown cords, all with lark's head knots. Reposition and clip the 39-inch (100 cm) strands at the top of the board to give them a "U" shape. Separate the cords into two equal groups.

STEP 2 Use the farthest-left thread as the holding cord to make a line of horizontal double half hitch knots from left to right into the center.

STEP 3 Repeat on the other side, and join both lines with a last double half hitch knot. Repeat this step two more times so as to get three lines on each side.

STEP 4 On the left side: Working from left to right, knot the strands in pairs, making a single vertical double half hitch knot. Repeat on the opposite side with knots from right to left.

STEP 5 On both sides, use the first holding threads to make a line with double half hitch knots, and join both lines in the middle with a last knot.

STEP 6 Make another line using the farthest-left and farthest-right threads as holding cords. You should end up with five lines in total.

STEP 7 Turn the knotting over to work on the back. Take a 16-inch (40 cm) navy-blue strand and tie it onto the first left thread using a simple overhand knot plus one vertical half hitch knot. Knot this cord around the next fifteen threads with vertical double half hitch knots. Use this same thread as the holding cord to make a brown line of horizontal double half hitch knots all the way to the middle. Repeat this step on the other side with a second navy-blue strand—don't forget to reverse the directions. Join both holding cords together.

STEP 8 On the front: Make one line on each side using the second nearest-right and second nearest-left threads as holding cords. Join them. Do not knot the navy-blue threads in the middle; leave them underneath the knotting.

STEP 9 On the back: Incorporate an 18-inch (45 cm) turquoise strand into the tenth left thread, and knot a turquoise row of vertical double half hitch knots to the middle. Do the same on the opposite side, then join both turquoise cords.

STEP 10 Turn over the weaving to make one last line on the front side. Use the next right and left threads just before the turquoise line as holding cords. Do not knot the turquoise threads when you join both browns at the center; leave them underneath.

STEP 11 Thread the beads onto the cords as shown here, or arrange them to your own design. Depending on the size and weight of the beads, you can string them on alternate strands.

STEP 12 Make two 10-inch (25 cm) braids with the 39-inch (100 cm) strands. Secure them at the end with overhand knots. C&M two of the three threads above the braids' knot as well as all the excess threads that remain around your knotting. Add the beads onto the third braid cord before doing a last overhand knot.

STEP 13 To finish your Stone Fringes Necklace, use a 10-inch (25 cm) turquoise thread to make a macramé sliding clasp around the braids (page 12).

Gwenaël Petiot was born in 1983 and raised in Aix-en-Provence, France. At age 15 he moved to Canada to play ice hockey. In 2001 he returned home to study lighting direction at audiovisual school. After working as an assistant lighting director in the television industry for a period, he quit his job in 2007 and traveled around South America. There Gwenaël discovered the craft that would become his passion— macramé. Needing to fund his adventures, he asked some Peruvian and Argentinian friends to teach him the secrets of macramé. He began by selling his creations on the street and earned sufficient money to travel for the next four years, visiting ten different countries, including Bolivia, Brazil, Ecuador, and Colombia.

Gwenaël returned to France in 2011 determined to use his newfound skills to earn a freewheeling living selling macramé jewelry. He went from selling his wares at craft markets around France to debuting his designs on the catwalk as part of the spring 2012 haute couture collection with French designer Anne Valérie Hash. Ever since, Gwenaël has sold his macramé designs at craft markets, online, and in shops under the name Papacho Creations. From time to time his remarkable creations can be seen adorning the famous Cirque du Soleil artistes.

He now lives in Paris and has never stopped enjoying the satisfaction of creating something amazing with knots and string.

A huge thanks to Lili, Stella, Coco, Nilton, Juan Carlos, and "los Salteños" for sharing their macramé techniques with me during my travels. Also a special thanks to Jo Bryant, Virginie, Mathieu, Tony, Mélanie B, Mélanie D, and particularly my family, who supported me when I decided to do macramé as a living.

Photography for the Cover and pages III, V, 16, 20, 24, 28, 34, 38, 42, 48, 54, 58, 64, 68, 78, 88, 92, 98, 104, 112, 122, 128 taken by Virginie Pérocheau